MILITARY
GEAR

Emma Bassier

DiscoverRoo
An Imprint of Pop!
popbooksonline.com

abdobooks.com

Published by Pop!, a division of ABDO, PO Box 398166, Minneapolis, Minnesota 55439. Copyright © 2020 by POP, LLC. International copyrights reserved in all countries. No part of this book may be reproduced in any form without written permission from the publisher. Pop!™ is a trademark and logo of POP, LLC.

Printed in the United States of America, North Mankato, Minnesota.

052019
092019

THIS BOOK CONTAINS
RECYCLED MATERIALS

Cover Photo: Shutterstock Images

Interior Photos: Shutterstock Images, 1, 12, 15 (bottom), 26, 30 (right), 31 (left), 31 (right); Defense Visual Information Distribution Service, 5, 8–9, 14, 17 (top), 17 (bottom), 20, 27; US Army, 6, 7; iStockphoto, 11, 16 (left), 21 (soldier), 24, 25, 30 (left); US National Archives and Records Administration, 13, 15 (top middle), 15 (top right); Library of Congress, 15 (top left), 16 (right); US Air Force, 19; US Marine Corps, 21 (camp); US Department of Defense, 23, 28–29

Editor: Connor Stratton
Series Designer: Jake Slavik

Library of Congress Control Number: 2018964855

Publisher's Cataloging-in-Publication Data

Names: Bassier, Emma, author.

Title: Military gear / by Emma Bassier.

Description: Minneapolis, Minnesota : Pop!, 2020 | Series: Inside the military | Includes online resources and index.

Identifiers: ISBN 9781532163845 (lib. bdg.) | ISBN 9781644940570 (pbk.) | ISBN 9781532165283 (ebook)

Subjects: LCSH: United States--Armed Forces--Equipment--Juvenile literature. | Military uniforms--Juvenile literature. | United States--Armed Forces--Uniforms--Juvenile literature.

Classification: DDC 623.4--dc23

WELCOME TO
DiscoverRoo!

Pop open this book and you'll find QR codes loaded with information, so you can learn even more!

Scan this code* and others like it while you read, or visit the website below to make this book pop!

popbooksonline.com/military-gear

*Scanning QR codes requires a web-enabled smart device with a QR code reader app and a camera.

TABLE OF
CONTENTS

CHAPTER 1
MILITARY GEAR IN ACTION

Eight soldiers are on a secret mission.

They crawl through a forest at night.

Night-vision goggles allow these soldiers

to see in the dark. The goggles pick up

kinds of light people cannot see.

WATCH A VIDEO HERE!

Then, the goggles change that light into

images people can see.

Night-vision goggles make
everything look green.

Can you spot all four soldiers?

The soldiers also have gear that
helps them hide. The whole squad wears
camouflage. Their jackets, pants, and
boots are brown and green. This color
pattern blends in with trees. It makes
it hard for enemies to spot the soldiers.

Woodland camouflage is green, brown, and black. Desert camouflage is tan and brown.

The US military started using desert camouflage in the 1980s.

The military uses lots of different gear. Soldiers use some gear for daily activities. Other gear is only useful for

Sailors check their supply of breathing tanks.

certain jobs. And some soldiers need

gear that other soldiers do not. But all

gear helps soldiers do their jobs.

CHAPTER 2
HISTORY OF MILITARY GEAR

Military gear has changed over time.

Armor is one example. Long ago, many soldiers wore chain mail. This armor was made by joining metal loops together. It protected soldiers in sword fights.

LEARN MORE HERE!

Chain mail was easier to move around in than other types of armor.

DID YOU KNOW? Thousands of years ago, Chinese warriors wore armor made of rhinoceros skin.

By the 1300s, fighting with guns had become more common. Soldiers needed armor that could stop bullets. So they tried using other materials. In the 1900s, people made armor from metal, fabric, or tough glass. The armor protected soldiers from **shrapnel**. But it still could not stop bullets.

A US soldier wears body armor in 1918.

In the 1980s, militaries began using Kevlar. This fabric is made from plastic. But it is strong enough to stop bullets. Kevlar body armor has saved many soldiers' lives.

Army helmets are often made with Kevlar.

From left to right: backpacks from 1861, 1918, and 2004

BETTER BACKPACKS

Soldiers' backpacks changed over time. Backpacks in the 1800s often had wooden backs. They were painful to use. Most soldiers carried their gear in a rolled blanket instead. In the 1900s, militaries began making backpacks from canvas. This fabric was light and comfortable. These backpacks became popular with soldiers.

MILITARY GEAR
TIMELINE

1000s BCE
Chinese warriors wear armor made of rhino skins.

1800s
Backpacks often have wooden backs.

1300s
Chain mail becomes less common as more armies begin using guns.

1900s
Soldiers wear camouflage uniforms and use backpacks made of canvas.

1980s

Soldiers use body armor made with Kevlar.

1950s

Soldiers use a lighter type of body armor.

1999

The US military uses a new sensor to find harmful chemicals in the air.

CHAPTER 3
MILITARY GEAR TODAY

Today, soldiers use many types of gear. Helmets protect soldiers' heads. A chin strap holds the helmet in place. Soldiers can also attach night-vision goggles to their helmets.

LEARN MORE HERE!

A soldier wears a helmet and night-vision goggles.

DID YOU KNOW?

Most US soldiers carry more than 60 pounds of gear. Soldiers with special jobs carry more.

Backpacks help soldiers carry other gear, such as a radio, traveling tools, and extra bullets. During trips, soldiers camp in tents. They drink from **canteens**. Their backpacks hold enough gear for 72-hour missions.

A soldier organizes the gear that will go in his backpack.

DID YOU KNOW? Military backpacks are sometimes called rucksacks or rucks.

MILITARY GEAR

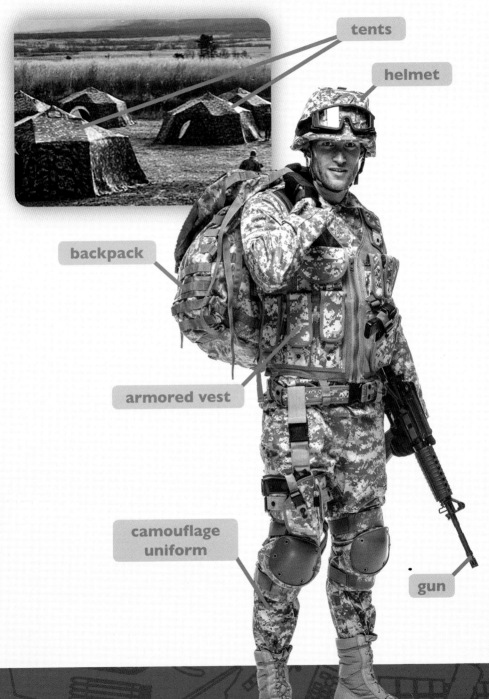

tents

helmet

backpack

armored vest

camouflage uniform

gun

CHAPTER 4
SPECIAL MILITARY GEAR

Soldiers use special gear for certain tasks. For many jobs, soldiers need **scopes** on their guns. These scopes project light onto the target. That light helps the soldier aim. Using scopes,

COMPLETE AN ACTIVITY HERE!

Some scopes can tell soldiers exactly how far away their target is.

soldiers can hit targets that are up to half

a mile away.

Snipers are highly skilled shooters. They try to hit targets without being seen or heard. Snipers often put bushrags on their guns. A bushrag is a **camouflage** cover. Fabric falls over the gun. It helps the gun stay hidden.

DID YOU KNOW?

A silencer is a tool that soldiers put on guns. It makes gunshots sound quieter.

A soldier uses a bushrag over his gun. Similar camouflage is on his body too.

Some gear helps soldiers search for danger. Mine detectors use sensors to study the ground. They find buried explosives. Chemical detectors test the air. They search for dangerous chemicals. They tell soldiers if the air is safe to breathe.

A Moroccan soldier uses a metal detector to check for explosives.

Soldiers wear masks if the air is

unsafe. The masks cover their eyes,

skin, and mouths. They stop smoke or

During training, soldiers practice using masks in rooms filled with poisonous gas.

chemicals from hurting soldiers. Soldiers

must be ready for many different

situations. Gear helps them prepare.

MAKING CONNECTIONS

TEXT-TO-SELF

What kind of military gear would you like
to try using? Why would you choose that kind?

TEXT-TO-TEXT

Have you read books about other kinds
of gear? How are they similar to and different
from military gear?

TEXT-TO-WORLD

Military gear helps soldiers on the battlefield.
Can you think of other places where these
tools could be helpful?

GLOSSARY

armor – a covering that protects the body.

camouflage – a pattern made to blend into its surroundings.

canteen – a metal or plastic water bottle used on trips.

mine – an explosive weapon often put underground.

scope – a device put on guns to help shooters with their aim.

shrapnel – bits of metal that fly through the air after an explosion.

INDEX

ONLINE RESOURCES

popbooksonline.com

Scan this code* and others like it while you read, or visit the website below to make this book pop!

popbooksonline.com/military-gear

*Scanning QR codes requires a web-enabled smart device with a QR code reader app and a camera.